The only publication that explains, from a
scientific viewpoint, the importance of fasting

GALA

EFFICACY OF FASTING

by

Dr. Dhiren Gala

B.Sc., D.H.M.S., D.O., D.Ac.,
C.G.O., C.C.H., A.R.S.H.

Recipient of a gold medal for extraordinary
work in the field of Alternative Therapeutics

With

Dr. D. R. Gala

N.D., D.N.O., D.C.O.

Dr. Sanjay Gala

M.B. (BOM.), M.S. (ENT)

NAVNEET PUBLICATIONS (INDIA) LIMITED

Navneet House	**Navneet Bhavan**
Gurukul Road, Memnagar,	Bhavani Shankar Road,
Ahmadabad – 380 052.	Dadar, Mumbai – 400 028.
Phone : 5530 5000	Phone : 6662 6565

DHANLAL BROTHERS DISTRIBUTORS

70, Princess Street, Mumbai – 400 002.

Phone : 2201 7027

G 4513

Visit us at : www.navneet.com   e-mail : npil@navneet.com   **Price : Rs. 15.00**

Dr. D. R. Gala

1st Floor, Abbas Building 'A',
Near Tilak Market, Jalbhai Lane,
Harkishandas Hospital Road,
Grant Road (East), Mumbai – 400 004.
Phone : 2386 7275
Time : 4.00 to 7.00 p.m.

PREFACE

There is no exaggeration in saying that 'fasting' has established its supremacy over other remedies in the treatment of a disease. All naturopaths corroborate this fact. It is a known fact that Mahatma Gandhi was a staunch advocate of fasting.

The occurrence of most diseases is due to improper dietetic habits and excessive eating. 'Our life is maintained on 25% of what we eat and on the remaining 75% live doctors'. Though the statement may appear a bit exaggerated, it is nevertheless true. There is no doubt that control over eating and occasional fasting when the need arises help us to maintain good health and help the diseased body to regain health.

In the modern age, man has been dazzled by scientific discoveries which give material comforts to mankind. Man now regards luxuries as the sole aim of life. As a consequence, he has forgotten the importance of fasting. Nobody dies on account of missing a meal or observing a day's fast. During the Paryushana festival of the Jains, even small children observe a fast of eight days without experiencing any ill-effects. There are cases in which people, thrown on to an uninhabited island or such other place, survived without eating anything for thirty to forty days or more.

There are a number of examples which show that health has improved after observing a fast scientifically. If one observes a fast properly, concludes it in a disciplined manner and thereafter resumes taking simple and nutritious diet gradually, one is sure to get the benefit of good health.

This book, though small in size, gives detailed scientific information about fasting and if the reader gets inspiration from it and puts into practice whatever he learns from it with a view to getting better health, he is sure to be benefitted.

This book has been written keeping in mind modern physiology and it gives complete scientific information about every aspect of fasting. We are confident that it will provide logical and authentic reading material to laymen, elites and medical men. Readers are requested to give their contribution to this humble endeavour by sending their views and letting us know their experiences.

– **Authors**

CONTENTS

1. THE MEANING AND THE PURPOSE OF FASTING

Taking food every day is man's common practice. Food helps him to sustain his life and continue doing his activities. He is said to have observed a fast on the day when he abstains from food for one reason or another. Fast has absolutely nothing to do with religion. It is true that on certain religious occasions we observe a fast by taking or abandoning certain food-items, but it cannot be called fasting in its true sense or from the scientific point of view. On the fast-day, compelled by religious sentiment, we keep control over our natural desire and avoid taking regular food (particularly made from cereals). However, in its substitution, we take other nutritious and heavy foods like milk and milk-products.

A fast means total abstention from taking any kind of food. It is essential not to take solid or liquid food, cereals, fruits and sometimes even water during a fast. A fast means absolute abstention from taking any kind of food for a definite period with a view to giving rest to the different organs of the body and their processes, thereby helping them to get cleansed. One may observe a fast by abstaining from food at one meal-time. It is called half-a-day fasting. One may observe a fast even by taking only fruits, fruit-juices or water. These are the different kinds of fasting, each with its special effect.

Some words commonly connected with fasting are deceptive. 'Water-fast' is one such word. Water-fast in literal sense would mean that water should not be drunk. But this meaning is false. The true meaning of 'water-fast' is only to drink water and except it not to take any food, fruit or milk. Fruit-fast and juice-fast are also such words. When a person abandons taking all food-items except fruits or fruit-juices, he is said to have observed a 'fruit-fast' or 'juice-fast'.

Fasting does not mean starving. Fasting and starving are two different conditions. It is true that in both the conditions food is not taken; however, as their causes and purposes are different, their meanings are also different. Fasting is a condition accepted voluntarily by an individual, while starvation is a condition arising out of circumstances (inability to get food) which are external and beyond the control of an individual.

There are two main functions of food : (1) to provide the body with nourishment and heat, (2) to produce new cells to take the place of the cells destroyed owing to depreciation caused by routine activities. The body stores some part of food, the nutrients of which are useful in some specific conditions.

During illness, the body uses its full energy in its fight against the disease. During this period as the body requires no particular nourishment, we feel a loss of appetite. During illness, the elimination of toxins and foreign elements from the body is of utmost importance. If food is taken during illness, precious energy is used up in digesting it.

When the body needs no nourishment, when it is necessary to remove toxins from the body and appetite is dormant, abstention from taking food is called fasting.

Even during a fast the body requires fuel or heat. For this purpose the body begins to burn toxic elements accumulated in it. Besides, the nutrients stored in the body are also useful for energizing the body. The organs or cells vital to the body are not destroyed for a long time during a fast.

Starvation is the condition in which the organs or cells vital to the body for its well-being are destroyed along with waste-products. If proper care is not taken, starvation will follow a fast kept for a long time. An expert physician puts a person who keeps a fast under his constant observation and as soon as he finds the symptoms of starvation, he advises the person to end his fast. The limit of the duration of a fast and the beginning of starvation have been scientifically discussed in the ensuing chapter.

'When a patient stops taking food, the disease and not the patient dies of starvation', this well known quotation by Dr. Dewey is true. As a matter of fact, in illness, food, instead of giving strength to a patient, nourishes and prolongs the disease.

The body needs definite food regularly. In the same way, it needs regular fasting at definite intervals. Food provides the body with energy and heat while a fast bestows health and purity on the body. Moreover, a fast gives rest to the various processes going on in the body such as digestion, blood-circulation, metabolism and revitalizes them.

Fasting is a never-failing therapy for those patients who have been disappointed by numerous medicines and therapies for the cure of their diseases. It is surprising that, while no improvement has been realized in the health of a number of patients even after they have been given modern medicines and treated with different therapies at many hospitals, the same patients get relief from disease by observing a fast of three to forty-five days.

A balanced-diet, according to the need of the body, following the rules regarding health and keeping a fast at definite intervals, helps an individual to maintain his good health. The therapy in which diseases are cured through prolonged fasting has been successful in the cases where diseases are deeply rooted in the body.

Observing birds and animals around us we may perhaps think that they never fall ill. But it is not true. Like human beings, birds and animals also fall ill; but the extent of illness among them is much less. When a bird or an animal falls ill, first of all it instinctively leaves food, i.e., observes a fast. It gets cured of its illness merely by observing a fast without any kind of medicine or therapy.

Thus, fasting effects a natural cure. If man follows it regularly, he can keep fit and remain healthy. A fast not only maintains health but can also cure most of the chronic diseases and many acute diseases. For the last one hundred and fifty years, the naturopaths and other health-reformers have accepted fasting as a sure treatment for the elimination of physical ailments. A fast is a positive energy which should be incorporated regularly and faithfully in modern life.

Those who understand the method of fasting and form the habit of regularly keeping a fast not only remain everhealthy but also disallow any disease to come near them.

2. FASTING : A SCIENTIFIC POINT OF VIEW

Fasting and starvation are two different conditions. A fast is observed when the body needs no food and going without food may possibly improve health. Starvation is a condition in which the body, though in need of food, does not get food. A fast is a saviour, while starvation is sometimes fatal. Fasting does not do any harm to the body, but it gives mental and physical health, while starvation leads one to death.

It is necessary to understand the limits of fasting and starvation. Starvation begins where fasting ends. A person who observes a fast, if enters the limit of starvation, invites the risk of damage to his body and health.

Some persons announce their desire to go on a fast of certain days. But, how long a fast would be required to eliminate a particular disease cannot be previously judged. It is, therefore, foolishness to previously decide the period of fasting. If a person observing a fast does not resume taking food even after entering the condition of starvation, he invites the risk of damage to his body and mind.

Special knowledge and experience are required to understand the deadline of fasting and the beginning of starvation. It is, therefore, necessary that a fast for a long period should be observed under the supervision of an expert physician.

To describe the difference between a fast and starvation is somewhat difficult for words. Nevertheless, we have tried to present their scientific aspects in a simple manner. Advantages of a fast and disadvantages of starvation have been explained here.

Below have been given the scientific reasons to show how a fast eliminates a disease and revives good health.

(1) **The digestive system gets rest :** A lot of energy of the body is used up in digesting the food taken. But when there is no function of digesting food, this energy gets a new direction. It is employed for eliminating a disease.

(2) **Elimination of toxins speeds up :** When the digestive system is at rest, the toxic elements accumulated in it get disintegrated. The natural curative power of the body takes up the task of removing these toxic elements from it. These toxins are gradually eliminated. Other remedies such as enema, steam-bath, hip-bath, hot foot-bath, Acupressure, Magnetotherapy etc. help make this elimination rapid.

(3) **The liver is activated :** The liver is the laboratory of the body. Whatever we eat is first of all digested by the processes of the digestive system. Then it gets absorbed in blood through mucous membrane of the intestines. The food thus digested reaches the liver through certain blood-vessels. Here it goes through a number of processes. The liver is the main organ which eliminates poisonous elements. Parenchymal cells of the liver begin to eliminate the poisonous elements of the food. As no food goes into the body during the period of fasting, new toxic elements are not produced. At such time these parenchymal cells of the liver use their full strength in the work of eliminating old toxins inhabited in the entire body. According to many researchers, the liver plays an important part in keeping the body healthy.

(4) **The resistance power increases :** When on account of fasting, toxic elements begin to be eliminated from the body, there is an increase in the natural resistance power of the body. Thus roused and revived, resistance power acquires the capacity for relieving the body of diseases. There is no exaggeration in saying that a strong resistance power of the body means extermination of a disease.

(5) **The mental power is enhanced :** It has been observed that most of the persons observing a fast, experiences the firmness of the mind and self-confidence during the fasting period. The development of mental power has a favourable influence on the body and therefore, relief from disease becomes easy.

The reasons for effectiveness of a fast have been discussed above; but how would one know when a fast ends and starvation begins ? Some doctors state that the 'feeling of hunger' is the factor that determines the deadline of fasting and the starting line and starvation respectively. This belief is fallacious and needs further consideration.

The hunger which a person feels during the first two or three days after the commencement of his fasting is habitual. It is not a real hunger. This false hunger vanishes after two or three days. A real hunger gets revived after the internal cleansing process of the body is completed. This condition indicates the deadline of fasting. Thereafter if food is not taken, starvation begins. It is very difficult to differentiate the end-line of fasting period and the initial-line of starvation on the sole basis of hunger sensation. Hunger is a subjective feeling. If one's mind is engaged in some interesting activity, one forgets the feeling of hunger. On the other hand, if one thinks of or sees a food-item of liking, one's hunger is awakened. So it will be a grave mistake to believe that starvation does not start till one feels really hungry. In the same way, if hunger is awakened by one reason or another, one should not believe that it is the deadline of fasting and the beginning of starvation.

In fact, the distinction between a fast and starvation should be judged on the basis of the findings of a certain laboratory investigations and the physician should have a thorough knowledge of the basic principles of human physiology.

During the period of fasting, the body, first of all, burns foreign elements and toxins in order to obtain nourishment. At the same time, catabolism of blood-sugar and fat begins to take place. If a fast is continued after fat is completely used up, the cells and the fibres of the organs useful to the body begin to disintegrate and the body derives its nourishment from them.

Ketone bodies are produced as the by-products of the catabolism of fat. These ketone bodies are absorbed in blood and make it acidic. As the disintegration of fat increases, blood becomes more and more acidic. If the proportion of ketone bodies in blood increases to more than 2.4 mg %, they even enter urine. This condition is known as ketonuria.

The presence of ketone bodies in urine is an alarming symptom, because ketosis leads to acidosis which puts life into a critical condition. Usually, this condition arises only after a prolonged fast, that is a fast of 40 to 50 days.

The person observing fast as well as the physician who is supervising his condition should be on the alert for any external symptom of acidosis. Nausea, vomitting, rapid and deep breathing (as if the patient is struggling for oxygen), irregular pulse, dehydration and changes in consciousness are some of the symptoms of acidosis.

As soon as one or more of these symptoms are evident, examination of urine becomes necessary.* The presence of ketone bodies in urine suggests that fasting should be ended.

It should be noted that the onset of ketosis and acidosis can be delayed if during fasting period one continues taking salts like soda or salt mixed with water or fruit-juices.

It is not, however, necessary that every person who fasts develops acidosis. If the person who keeps a fast is lean and has negligible quantity of fat in his body, he may suffer from disintegration of proteins without being affected by ketosis and this may prove fatal to his life.

The disintegration of proteins gradually increases the proportion of urea in blood. The normal proportion of urea in blood is 15 to 45 mg %. If the proportion measures more

---

* Chemical analysis of urine by Rothera's or Gerhart's metho
  the concentration of ketone bodies in it.

than that (a condition called uremia), urea starts spilling into the urine. If this is found out by laboratory investigations, fasting should immediately be discontinued.

In short, a fast of ten to twelve days is completely safe. A person having a good amount of fat in his body, with due care, can safely and fearlessly observe a fast of 30 or a few more days. Fasting more than this limit needs the supervision and observation of an expert physician. Those who are slim and who suffer from diseases emaciating their body are advised not to observe a fast of more than 8 to 10 days.

Any person can keep a fast and derive its benefits provided his condition is under constant observation and body periodically checked.

3. BEFORE FASTING

One, who desires to keep a fast of short or long duration, should first of all determine the purpose or object of fasting. What one desires to achieve or what accomplishment does one long for by observing a fast should be clarified at the outset. Fasting is generally kept for the removal of physical ailments. In some cases prolonged fasting is planned to get rid of chronic diseases. Moreover, sometimes one takes resort to fasting also for mental peace and spiritual progress. One who observes a fast should have a clear conception as regards the aim and purpose of fasting. Then one should determine to observe the fast and firmly stick to that determination. A fast observed with full faith and self-confidence undoubtedly gives expected benefits.

Is any preparation necessary prior to the beginning of fast ? This question is important. No specific preparation is necessary for a fast of one or two days or even for a weekly fast. Specific preparations, however, are necessary before starting a fast of a longer duration.

First of all, a person desirous of fasting should procure all basic and scientific information regarding fasting. This type of information is available from the books on fasting or from some physician. This will help him to know the right method of fasting and the rules to be observed during a fast. The information also allays the fear or misconception about fasting. Once the person gets faith in the process of fasting, he comes to know of its benefits. This makes him mentally cheerful and emboldens him to observe a fast.

One should get some prior experience with a fast of short duration that is of one or two days as a preparation before observing a fast of long duration. This will give courage and firmness to one in one's determination.

The body requires complete rest during fasting. Light, mental activities should be previously planned in order to save one from boredom during fasting. Good reading, prayers and other such activities may be included in the plan.

It is necessary that the person who fasts should get the co-operation from the members of his family during fasting. For this, he should inform all the members of his family about his desire to fast and assure himself of their co-operation. Mental peace and self-confidence are of utmost importance during this period. If the members of the family oppose to one's fasting, their opposition may cause mental affliction and agony. In such cases, expected benefits may not be gained. In case there is no hope of getting co-operation from the members of the family, one desirous of fasting should take resort to a nature-cure centre. There, fasting becomes easy and smooth on account of natural surroundings and presence of other fasting persons.

Simple, light and nutritious food should be taken for five to seven days before the beginning of a fast of long duration. Raw vegetables, sprouted pulses and sprouted cereals should be taken in large quantities. These food-items are full of vitamins and minerals which help in eliminating toxic elements inhabited in the body. In addition to this benefit, the surplus vitamins and minerals, which one gets from the above food-items, are stored in the body which are later useful to the body during the fasting period.

Simple and natural remedies, if applied for the cure of a disease a few days prior to the beginning of a fast, prove beneficial to a faster.

Cleanliness of bowels is necessary before beginning a fast. Mild purgatives like 'harade' (terminalia chebula) or isabgol (plantago ovator) or enema will be helpful in getting the bowels cleansed. This should be remembered on the first day of the fast. Stool lying in the intestine dries up and its poisonous elements are absorbed in the body which damage the functioning of the body or delay the cure of a disease. Enema is also necessary two or three days after the beginning of a fast.

It is not desirable to fix the period of fasting before beginning a fast, because the period of fasting depends on necessity and circumstances.

In short, there is no doubt in the success of fasting which is begun with complete consciousness, faith and after proper preparations.

4. WHAT SHOULD A FASTER DO DURING HIS FASTING PERIOD ?

It is of prime importance that during fasting one should stick firmly to the aim, faith, self-confidence and desire to get result for which one has undertaken fasting. A fast is not only a physical process but also a mental process of a higher stratum. It is, therefore, essential to follow certain physical and mental rules during the entire fasting period. A faster would get the maximum benefits and get rid of diseases and regain health provided he strictly follows the rules mentioned below :

Physical rules : (1) The faster should drink as much water as possible during the period of fasting. A glassful of lukewarm water should be taken three or four times a day. Cold water may be drunk at intervals; but it should be remembered that instead of drinking a large quantity of water at a time, small doses of water should be drunk at intervals. Water is a medium that dissolves toxic elements and poisons produced in the body. The body is then able to discard from itself such dissolved poisons.

The first dose of water to be taken in the morning should be mixed with lemon juice and a little honey. Thereafter, juices of citrus and sweet fruits or a small quantity of salt or soda-bi-carb may be added to water twice or thrice a day. This helps to maintain the supply of salts to the body and prevents acidosis which generally occurs during the period of fasting. The salts and the vitamins derived from fruit-juices also help in cleansing the body.

(2) Enema should be taken at an interval of every two or three days so that stool may not be accumulated in the large intestine and absorbed by it. If the stool begins to be absorbed in the intestine, its poisonous elements mix with blood. To prevent this condition, the bowels should be completely evacuated, if necessary, by an enema.

(3) The faster should take a bath with tepid or lukewarm water every day to remove foul-smelling perspiration. If he feels weakness, he should get his body sponged by some acquaintance.

(4) The faster should always live in open, clean air. Deep-breathing is beneficial to a faster. Even in cold season, a faster should take the advantage of open air. He can wear woollen clothes, if necessary.

(5) A sun-bath early in the day is beneficial to the faster. He should sit, with his bare body, in the morning sunshine for half an hour. This can be repeated in the evening, if desired.

(6) A poultice of wet-clay should be put on the abdomen once a day. It is important to do this when the stomach is empty.

(7) During the period of fasting, the faster should simultaneously undertake natural physical measures such as massage, hip-bath, steam-bath and hot foot-bath.

(8) The faster should avoid doing any activity which would entail jerky or rapid movements. During the period of fasting, the concentration of sugar in the blood decreases. Hence too rapid, laborious or jerky activities may cause undue fatigue or giddiness.

Mental rules : A faster would get more and quick benefits if he practises the following mental rules during the period of fasting :

(1) Think positively and constructively during fasting. Stick firmly to your determination of achieving good health and continue your efforts till you get the expected result. Remember that a disease is the consequence of incorrect dietary habits and life-style, and fasting is an atonement for these bad habits.

(2) Remain cheerful throughout the period of fasting. Live a life of hope, delight and joy. Do not get angry. Avoid despair and worries. Do not be disappointed. Anger, worry, despair and disappointment are the factors which are impediments to health. Keep away from them. Cheerfulness, firmness and self-confidence are the steps which lead you to health. Also do not allow fear or fright to overcome you.

(3) During the period of fasting, concentrate on such thoughts as would sublimate your mind. Have rosy dreams. Read such books as would give you peace and inspiration. Listen to music and say prayers.

(4) If possible, try to stay alone, in isolation, during the period of fasting. Keep away from noise pollution. Try to avoid the contact of those persons who do not know anything about the beneficial effects of a fast. This is because the talks of such persons may shake your faith and infuse fear in you regarding a fast.

(5) Keep your senses away from the sight of food and its fragrance. Drive away the thoughts of food from your mind. Forget the kitchen. Do not talk anything about food.

(6) Do not worry yourself about annoyance, idleness, weakness, insomnia, headache etc., the feelings you will experience for two or three days in the beginning of the period of fasting. All these discomforts will rapidly vanish if you have firmness and self-confidence.

Discomforts during fasting : It is possible that the faster may experience some discomforts during fasting. Naturopaths consider these discomforts as good signs. According to them, discomforts are the signs or symptoms showing that the vitality of the body has increased and the body is being cleansed. If the faster is aware of possible discomforts produced during fasting, such discomforts do not frighten him. His confidence in fasting sustains and he does not abandon fasting before the completion is due.

A one-day fast causes no discomfort. No particular trouble ensues even during a three-days fast. It is only the mind that craves for food. The faster also experiences depression and indolence. Mental causes are also responsible for the weakness which is felt by the faster in more or less proportions. If the faster commences his fasting after proper preparations, he feels energetic and not weak. He feels that his body has become light.

With the commencement of fasting, foreign and toxic elements inhabited in the different parts of the body begin to disintegrate. Within three days, these toxic elements begin to enter blood and influence the brain and the nerves. At this time, the faster feels slight weakness.

The persons in whose bodies toxic elements have been accumulated in great quantities may have to face certain ailments. An expert physician should plan fasting in such a way that the faster would suffer minimum weakness and ailments.

The following ailments may occur during the period of fasting :

(1) The sense of taste deteriorates.

(2) The tongue becomes filthy.

(3) The colour of urine becomes deep.

(4) Nausea-vomitting occurs.

(5) At the time of doing an activity involving jerks, the faster feels giddiness and his vision becomes blurred.

(6) The faster suffers insomnia or gets sleep less than required.

(7) At times the faster may suffer from diarrhoea, fever, rapid beating of the heart, etc.

All these ailments except the last are not worth worrying. If the faster suffers from palpitation, quick and deep breathing or unconsciousness, the chemical test of urine becomes inevitable. If necessary, the fast may be terminated in such conditions.

If the faster is under the observation of an expert and experienced physician, he should not worry about the ailments mentioned above. These ailments occur suddenly and also vanishes suddenly. The disappearance of ailments signifies that the processes of detoxification and cleansing of the body have been completed.

5. HOW SHOULD FASTING BE ENDED

Compared to pre-fasting period, the post-fasting period calls for much greater care and patience. It has also a scientific importance. The conclusion of fasting requires patience and discretion. If necessary, an expert physician's advice may be solicited.

When a fasting person feels genuinely hungry, his tongue is clean and without stickiness and he feels the sense of taste and saliva in his mouth, he should realize that all those are the signs for him to end his fasting. They should be considered ideal symptoms. The feelings of weakness and dejection should not be considered seriously at this juncture. If the circumstances demand, the fasting may be ended earlier than the determined period.

Meal is to be taken at the end of fast. It is more important than the fast itself. Sometimes it so happens that the faster may not realize expected benefits during fast. But he experiences these benefits within a few days after the end of the fast.

More care and caution are required when the person brings an end to his fasting. Patience and self-control are of vital importance at this critical time.

Benefits derived through fasting become long-lasting only when proper care is taken at the end of fasting. This proper care also saves one from having to repeat fasting.

When the person ends his fast he should remember that his digestive system has been inactive during the period of fasting. Glands connected with the digestion have been in dormant condition. The intestines have temporarily shrunk in size. Under this situation, the faster should have patience. Great care should be taken before burdening these weakened digestive organs with the work of digesting food. The digestive organs should be allowed to function gradually and in order.

Experts advise that at the time of ending fast, only a little quantity of juices of sweet and citrus fruits like orange and lemon should be taken. At the initial stage there should be a long interval between the two takings of fruit-juices. This duration may be shortened gradually with an increase in the quantity of fruit-juices. After ending the fast and taking the first dose of fruit-juices, it is desirable that bowels are evacuated after three or four hours. If this does not happen naturally, enema should be resorted to.

At the initial stage, liquid food like fruit-juice or vegetable-juice should be taken for two to four days. The quantity of liquid food should be as little as possible which may be increased gradually. After four or five days, juicy and soft fruits, boiled vegetables and a little quantity of dried fruits may be taken. In ordinary circumstances, a faster should allow long time to elapse before he resumes eating cooked food.

It is not only madness but also thoughtless and harmful to take nourishing and fatty foods immediately after ending a fast of long duration, hoping to regain rapidly energy and weight lost during the fast. The food to be taken after ending the fast should be completely controlled. It is desirable that after a long fast, there should be an interval of about 15 days to one month before the resumption of taking usual food. If this rule is not strictly followed, fasting becomes not only meaningless but may also have adverse effects on the body and the mind.

The necessity of fasting arises only when regularity, propriety and proportion are not maintained in eating and drinking. Therefore, if irregularity, impropriety and thoughtlessness in eating and drinking are resumed after fasting, the body again becomes a store-house of toxins and poisonous elements which cause diseases.

Fasting is merely a timely remedy which leads to health. A person who is regular in his eating and drinking and who lives a controlled life, rarely needs fasting of long duration. It is enough for him to take a fast or miss a meal once a week or a fortnight.

Some persons feel weakness and flaccidity for about a week after the fast is concluded. This is a strange phenomenon which lasts only for a short time. This weakness disappears as soon as the blood sugar level rises to the normal values.

An increase in the temperature of the body or fever after giving up the fast is the result of haste or carelessness in the resumption of taking food. However, it should not be a matter of undue worry. If such a condition arises, the quantity of food should be reduced or a fresh fast of a day or two should be observed.

One should take rest for about a week after the end of the fast. Physical exertion should follow gradually. At the time of becoming active again after fasting, one should take into consideration the condition of one's body and one's experiences.

6. FASTING : WHERE AND WHEN ?

Materialism is growing fast in the modern age. We are so much fascinated by it that in following it we forget to take care of our health and body. There is a great change in our habits of eating and drinking. Today, it appears that we live to eat. Everybody runs after luxuries. In these circumstances, who would think of a fast ? The scene of health is becoming gloomy day by day. There is a remarkable increase in illnesses and diseases. The search for new medicines and remedies is incessantly going on. Most people today are under the illusion that modern medicines can cure any disease of the body. Under such circumstances, who would readily agree to keep a fast ?

But it is a fact that those who have been tired of medicines and disappointed by the modern therapy have now begun to turn to nature cure. There is a continuous increase in the number of persons who desire to gain health and become free from diseases through fasting.

These people face two questions :

Where should they fast ? When should they fast ?

A nature cure centre is the ideal place where a person can fast, because here the faster has congenial (favourable) atmosphere, necessary facilities and inspiration. Besides, an expert physician's advice is always easily available here. In a nature cure centre, there are facilities for hip-bath, steam-bath, massage etc. in addition to the services of expert physicians. The atmosphere, climate and environment of a nature cure centre are very congenial to the faster. Here he can get the company of other fasters also which gives mental peace and patience to him.

Some persons try to observe a fast at home, living with the members of the family. But they fail to get expected success. As other members of the family do not know anything about fasting, they frequently advise the faster to give up fasting or express possibilities of having adverse effects of fasting. They show him delicious food and insist on his taking it. Consequently, the faster becomes weak in his determination and loses his faith in fasting. He becomes unsteady. He suffers from a mental conflict. Thus, his determination and method of fasting falter, resulting into a great damage.

The faster needs inspiring and cheerful atmosphere and co-operation of the members of the family for the success of his fasting. If these situations are not available at home, he should unhesitatingly take shelter of a nature cure centre.

The other problem which the faster faces concerns with time. The process of fasting is closely connected with climate and atmosphere. It is, therefore, to be considered which season is most suitable and beneficial for observing a fast.

In winter or cold season, fats stored under the skin of the body of the faster are used up for nourishment. During the period of fasting, the faster loses his capacity to bear cold. It is, therefore, natural that the faster would feel more cold in winter. Hence, it is advisable to keep a fast in summer or hot season.

It may happen sometimes that a person is in urgent need of keeping a fast in winter only. Should he wait and postpone fasting till summer ? No. If circumstances necessitate a person to keep fasting in winter, he may observe a fast also in winter provided he takes all possibe precautions to protect himself from cold. In the event of any difficulty, one who is an expert in fasting or a physician should be consulted.

If fasting is necessary to get relief from some illness and if it is postponed till summer, illness may grow and take a serious turn. Thus, it is possible that an ordinary disease in winter may turn into a serious or an incurable disease by summer.

Hence, in inevitable circumstances, there is no risk in fasting with all possible cares and cautions against cold. Necessary arrangements should, however, be made to keep the faster's body warm.

It is not necessary to follow these rules strictly when a fast is of a short period of a day or two.

---

7. FASTING AND DISCRIMINATION

The main purpose of fasting is to get relief from diseases and regain health. However, opinions differ in considering a fast as an acceptable remedy for every disease in all conditions. It has not yet been definitely concluded whether fasting can cure all diseases or its efficacy is restricted only to certain diseases.

Experts and physicians clearly state that fasting is not an antidote to all diseases. It is, however, an undisputed fact that fasting is the most effective remedy for the cure of most of diseases. There is hardly a disease which will not be cured partially or completely by fasting unless the organs of the body are totally inactive or the resistance power of the body is completely worn out.

The tendency to opt for a fast in each and every physical or mental illness is also not good. Fasting should be used as a cure only after the symptoms and condition of a disease are truly diagnosed. Fasting should never be used as a cure without consulting a physician.

The information regarding the diseases and physical conditions in which fasting should not be observed is given below :

(1) **During pregnancy :** During pregnancy, the mother and the developing foetus require more nourishment. It is, therefore, desirable not to keep a fast during this period. Pregnant women, instead, of fasting may accept the regimen of fruit-juices and controlled food-items.

(2) **In cancer :** Fasting is not effective when cancer is extensively spread. Benefits of fasting claimed in some cancer-cases are merely accidental (contingent). Only the diet of fruit-juices can give some benefits in the illness of cancer.

(3) **In tuberculosis :** Malnutrition is one of the causes of tuberculosis. Thus, a person suffering from T.B. is considered to be suffering from starvation. He should, therefore, not be advised to keep a fast.

(4) There is a deficiency of certain necessary elements in the body when a person suffers from scurvy, beri-beri, pellagra, rickets, night-blindness, keratomalacia, marasmus, kwashiorkor syndrome, etc. So he should not be advised to keep a fast in these conditions.

(5) As there is deficiency of secretions of the internal glands in diseases like thyrotoxicosis and hyper-adrenalism, a person suffering from such diseases should not keep a fast.

(6) The body loses much of its protein in the diseases of liver and kidneys. So a person suffering from either of the diseases should not be advised to keep a fast.

Excepting the above-mentioned diseases, fasting is a sure remedy for all other minor or major diseases. Fasting certainly yields benefits. It is true that in chronic diseases it takes a long time to get the desired benefits.

No sane person will ever believe that the health once achieved through fasting will last for ever. To maintain good health one has to be moderate in his habits of eating and drinking and should strictly follow other health-rules. Physical exercise, hard work, yogasanas and mental cheerfulness are equally necessary. Moreover, a fast of a day every week and a fast of three or four days every year should regularly be observed.

Fasting is merely a treatment for eliminating toxic and foreign elements produced in the body. It is, therefore, wrong to believe that a fast once kept would maintain good health for ever.

To maintain invaluable health achieved through fasting, one should always be cautious and careful to see that toxic elements do not again accumulate in the body; and, in case such a thing happens, one should be prepared to fast again in order to eliminate toxins from the body.

8. FASTING FOR MENTAL AND SPIRITUAL DEVELOPMENT

From ancient times, fasting has been given importance not only for physical health but also for mental and spiritual health. Long term fasting observed by great saints like Jesus Christ, Mohammad Paigambar and Mahavir are the examples of spiritual fasting. In Jainism, such fasts are popular. Mahatma Gandhiji also observed long fasts with the same view.

If a correct picture of the mental condition of a faster during the period of fasting be presented to the people, they will welcome fasting with more respect. This will undoubtedly allay the fear of fasting usually felt by the people.

If, during the period of fasting, a faster takes enough rest and avoids doing laborious work, he does not experience weakness. Several cases have been recorded showing that fasters, after a few days of fasting, have experienced more energy than they had before fasting. There are two main reasons for this : The first reason is that as the faster stops taking food, the body burns toxic and foreign substances contained in it in order to get nourishment for itself. Thus, the body begins to be purified and the faster feels himself fresh and energetic on account of the elimination of toxins. The other reason is that during the period of fasting, the faster achieves mental peace and firm determination. It is an undisputed fact that the mind is one of the important causes of strength or weakness.

According to experienced fasters, thoughts become steady and pure during the period of fasting. Complete peace and joy pervade the mind and the faster experiences (attains) spiritual joy. Shree Anandvardhanji says that the persons who have described spiritual joy must have remained in the condition of fasting. If man wills, he can be one with God within a few moments through fasting. Man's mind naturally inclines to God during the period of fasting and the light of divine knowledge spreads in his heart.

Dr. Edward Purington, the author of "The Philosophy of Fasting", states that physical health can be gained by various nature cure methods. But for mental health, fasting has no alternative. According to his opinion, fasting makes the sense-organs energetic and enables one to get control over unsteadiness of the mind. Fasting helps to develop such of virtues as peace of the mind, confidence, courage and respect. Fasting awakens natural instincts that formerly remained dormant. Thus, the faster morally and spiritually begins to rise to sublimity.

The faster, even after abandoning fasting, shows no inclination to improper food. His entire life and mode of living are changed. Ultimately, his life becomes sublime and healthy.

9. WEIGHT REDUCTION THROUGH FASTING

It is a matter of regret that there is no place for physical exertion in the present style of modern life. People have now inclined to take meals full of spices. As a consequence, most of these persons suffer from obesity today. Obesity is not merely a condition of the body but a disease. With the passing of time, obesity becomes the source of several diseases.

However, there is a remarkable increase in the number of persons being conscious of the dangers involved in obesity. Many persons now desire to reduce the weight of their body. They apply different treatments after consulting medical men, physicians and experts. These treatments include anorexiants, other medicines, physical exercises, etc.

Many persons try to reduce their obesity by restricting certain food-items but rarely get the expected results. There are certain reasons for this. First of all, the process of weight reduction is very slow. Secondly, strict regimen is required for observing rules regarding restricted food-items. To eat less is more difficult than not to eat at all. Thirdly, as the process involves a restricted diet for a long duration, an ordinary man is unable to sustain such an ordeal for a long time. It is true that restricted regimen accepted for a few days helps to reduce some kilos but old habits, revive as soon as the regimen is over, and the person resumes eating those food-items which he was used to taking formerly. Consequently, the weight begins to increase. We rarely find a fat man living on a restricted diet for a long time.

One gets more and sure success in reducing one's weight by fasting than by a restricted diet, and that also in a short span of time. The arguments of some doctors that fasting is nothing but starvation or it is injurious to health are fallacious. If a slim person can observe a fast safely, an obese person can do so more safely. It is, however, desirable that prolonged fasting should be undertaken under the observation of an experienced physician.

The following are the benefits of fasting kept with a view to reducing weight :

(1) It reduces the weight of the body without damaging health.

(2) Fasting gives more joy than the taking of restricted food, because in fasting there is no feeling of false appetite.

(3) Fasting has no adverse effects on the muscles or the skin. The skin loses neither smoothness nor elasticity.

The signs of improved health are manifested as the body begins to lose weight. They are :

(1) Respiration becomes easier than before.

(2) All the activities of the body become normal and natural.

(3) The body feels freshness and energy.

(4) The feeling of fatigue vanishes.

(5) There is no pain in abdomen.

(6) Blood pressure comes down and the heart seems to become more efficient.

(7) Seeing the weight being reduced, one experiences the feeling of joy and contentment.

The proportion of daily weight reduction depends on individual physical condition and circumstances. In the fasting of long period, the body loses about three quarters to one kg weight daily. There is no possibility of any damage to the body if this proportion of daily weight reduction is maintained.

If one desires to reduce the weight faster and if one is healthy, one may resort to some physical exercises along with fasting. To reduce the weight of particular parts of the body, definite asanas are of much use. Light or moderate physical exercises may be resorted to. There should be a regular planning for physical exercises. Heavy physical exercises are not desirable, for they stimulate hunger.

Some may argue that physical exercise or exertion alone can reduce the weight; but experiences have convinced that it takes a very long time for reducing the weight. More exercises are needed for the purpose. A common man does not have strength and patience required for that much physical exertion. Splitting wood for ten and a half hours or horse-riding of forty-three miles can reduce only half a kg of weight.

To conclude, for weight reduction fasting has no alternative. Fasting not only reduces obesity and weight of the body but it purifies the body and begets health also. After the conclusion of fasting, putting into practice the rules of eating and drinking as well as avoiding over-eating are also equally necessary.

---

10. FASTING INCREASES ENERGY

It is true that the weight of the body is reduced by fasting of either short duration or long duration; but it is absolutely wrong to say that fasting reduces the energy of the body or makes the body devitalized. From the experiences of innumerable men and women, it has been noted that fasting of long duration increases energy instead of decreasing it. On the other hand, the patients who are given good, nutritious and energizing food under the guidance of physicians are found losing their strength, energy and stamina day by day. But when these patients observe a fast, their energy begins to increase rapidly. Such occurrences may appear strange or full of exaggeration, but it has scientific reasons. Neither the decreased quantity of food nor the lack of nutrients in food is the cause of an individual's weakness. People become victims of debility and weakness on account of the accumulation of toxic elements and foreign substances in the body. As fasting eliminates all these undesirable and harmful substances from the body, the latter gets revitalized and the faster feels energetic and enthusiastic.

Those having debility and less weight constantly worry about their body. Such people resort to nutritious food and medicines in order to develop their body, increase weight and gain strength. They also do physical exercises. Even after this, if they do not get encouraging results, they begin to take more food. But this method of regaining health and strength is quite improper. The belief that the body can be made strong by taking nourishing food in more quantity is erroneous.

In the case when the patient's body is worn out, he is too weak to change the sides in bed, suffers from pain and unable to digest food. More food given to him increases his ailments instead of decreasing them. There is a possibility of an increase in his debility.

In the modern age, various foods and drinks are so entwined with man that he is unable to do without them even for a couple of hours. He feels that he cannot keep up his spirit and mood without a cup of tea or coffee and his body will wear and become weak without tasty and nutritious food. To get himself rid of this unreal fear, he takes snacks twice or thrice a day, heavy meals twice a day and cold or hot drinks several times a day. Despite loss of appetite, nausea, uneasiness or sleepiness, man is not contented without foods or drinks.

Such improper foods and drinks alone have made and continue to make modern man weak, worn out and worthless. To keep himself away from suffering such a pitiable plight, man takes various types of medicines, the result of which is nevertheless unsatisfactory.

There is a sure increase in one's physical strength during and after long, systematic fasting. If a person, who is weak, ill and dying is persuaded to discontinue medical treatment and other treatments and made to fast with his proper understanding, not only his illness disappears but also his life becomes rejuvenated with new energy and vitality.

Many persons do a lot of physical exertion during the period of their fasting. Some fasters have become winners in the running race. Others have achieved world-records in weight-lifting. Most of the fasters go on with their physical and mental activities for a long time and yet they do not experience any kind of discomfort.

After a fast, the body realizes its true strength, the mind experiences astonishing vitality, and physical as well as mental activities are performed with increased efficiency and speed. Every faster unfailingly gets such experiences.

------

11. REJUVENATION BY FASTING

At present, various kinds of researches are being made to discover a remedy for stopping old age or aging process. For this, drugs, exercises, yogasanas and other experiments are suggested. A significant success has been achieved in preventing old age through nature cure.

Possibilities of regaining complete youth are comparatively very less in the cases of persons having attained too old age. It is, however, possible to check the quickness of the aging process by fasting. A condition of old age during youth can certainly be prevented. Definite results can be achieved by removing its causes.

Old age is the result of a gradual accumulation of waste-products and poisonous substances in the body. A prevention of the production of these poisonous substances or their regular elimination has no adverse effect on the cells of the body and the cells attain long life. Despite cellular division and redivision going on continuously in the body, the cells are hardly destroyed. This process checks aging process and death can possibly be delayed for a long time.

There is no truth in the belief that it is difficult to maintain youth after the age of thirtyfive or forty. There is no particular reason why at this age, the muscles of the body cannot be improved after bringing necessary changes in them.

Fasting makes all this possible. There is no exaggeration in the statement that the body can be rejuvenated by fasting.

New and pure blood begins to flow in the blood-vessels immediately after fasting. Freshness and youth are reborn. Every organ of the body enjoys new strength and energy. Vitality which has been so far dormant begins to wake up, sluggishness and debility disappear, much strength and divine peace are experienced, the mind becomes alert and cheerful. All these are undoubtedly the features of youth. After fasting the mental condition very rapidly improves along with the physical condition. Deafness disappears, the eyes sparkle with new lustre, the nose and the tongue regain their natural power. The organs which have shrunk by the diseases like paralysis regain new life. The digestive system and the intestines get back their lost strength. As the wrinkles on the body and the face disappear, the colour of the body attains new lustre. The body assumes the colour of copper with the new flow of blood in it. The disorders in the mouth disappear. Blood-pressure decreases. There is a healthy improvement in the functioning of the heart and the efficiency of the lungs.

Fasting of long or short duration as per requirement makes these changes possible.

As a matter of fact, we are reborn because of fasting. Poisonous substances accumulated in the body and worn out cells being eliminated are replaced by new cells. Fasting activates the functioning capacity of all the organs of the body so much that it lasts for a long time even after fasting has been abandoned.

The cells in the body continuously undergo the processes of disintegration, reconstruction, depreciation and repairs. One process destroys the cell (catabolism), while the other process produces the new cells (anabolism). The sum of these processes is known as metabolism. Catabolism takes place when the body is active, while anabolism takes place when the body is at rest.

The process of catabolism is quicker during the initial period of fasting. The process of anabolism is activated before the end of fasting. Nature has endowed the body with power to destroy worn cells and produce new ones to take their place. The body is capable to reconstruct the cells.

It is an undisputable fact that rejuvenation is possible if, after fasting, one takes fruit and vegetable juices, does exercises and yogasanas regularly, meditates and forms the habit of remaining ever cheerful.

12. FASTING : A FEW CASES

No other treatment of diseases is as simple as fasting, yet it is effective against most diseases. There will be no reason for disappointment if one resorts to fasting with complete understanding and faith. Excepting a few illnesses, almost all illnesses can be cured with the help of fasting. The best thing about fasting is that besides the main disease (for which it is resorted to), it also beneficially affects other minor ailments which that person happens to suffer from. Fasting works as a panacea. A number of cases have been recorded in the different parts of the world showing the efficacy of fasting. It is not possible to include the description of each of them in this booklet. However, a few cases worth mentioning have been described briefly here as illustrations.

1. FASTING CAUSES NO WEAKNESS

People generally believe that the existence of strength in the body is dependent on food intake only, and missing even a single meal causes weakness. This belief has no base, as weakness is connected more with disease than lack of food.

Seven days' fasting observed by Dr. Bernarr MacFeddan, a strong advocate of fasting, has been well publicized for the prupose of mitigating people's above-mentioned conviction. During his seven days' fasting, Doctor MacFeddan used to walk for about ten miles every day. On the seventh day of his fasting, he demonstrated his strength in public by raising up a man whose weight was 200 lbs. Thus he established the fact that physical strength could be maintained during the period of fasting.

2. FASTING UPTO A MONTH IS NOT HARMFUL

Unless there is any particular physical trouble, a month's fasting is not at all harmful. The case of Dr. Gustav Gayer who observed a fast of 31 days in May, 1910 establishes this fact.

Doctor Gayer was an ardent advocate of fasting. In his time, fasting had not gained much popularity in America. Fasting was considered to be useless. So in order to prove the usefulness and safety of fasting, Doctor Gayer decided to observe a long fast in public.

During his fasting he invited Dr. W. Young, Dr. Floid Anist, Dr. A. B. Jameson, Dr. J. S. Vile (Pathologist) and Dr. M. H. Curvey (Neurologist), five eminent doctors of New York, to examine his body at regular intervals of time.

Doctor Gayer did not make any change in his routine activity even after he had begun his fasting. He kept himself engaged regularly in his activities.

He was a professor at a medical college. He continued to give lectures at the college daily. He also continued to examine his private patients and treat them. Thus, he continued to utilize all his physical energy.

On the twelfth day of his fasting, a newspaper reporter called on him. The reporter had thought that Doctor Gayer might be in bed due to weakness and unable to talk. But to his surprise, he found that what he had anticipated was wrong. He published the report on Doctor Gayer's condition as found on the twelfth day and thereafter in his newspaper. The report is as follows :

"On the twelfth day of his fasting neither weakness nor indolence was least found in Doctor Gayer. Not only was he engrossed in his activity but also he was humming songs joyfully. He ascended and descended the staircase quite speedily. The speed of his walking was also noteworthy."

There was no signficant change in his condition even on the seventeenth day of his fasting. Doctor Anist of New York Board of Health examined him and stated that his muscle strength was intact. Doctor Gayer demonstrated that he could raise a chair weighing 25 lb. with his one hand. According to Doctor Anist, no harm was caused to Doctor Gayer's body because of his abstinence from food.

On the twentieth day of his fasting, Doctor Vile examined Doctor Gayer's blood and reported that the blood was completely healthy and normal. The number of red corpuscles was quite normal.

On the twenty-third day of fasting, Doctor Curvey stated that Doctor Gayer's nervous system is quite in order and he is alert. His intelligence was also found very sharp.

On the twenty-fifth day of fasting, Doctor Young examined Doctor Gayer and stated that Doctor Gayer appeared like a living symbol of health. His pulse (heart-beats), his body temperature and all the systems of his body were found normal.

Doctor Gayer concluded his fast on the 31st day. He could remain active as before even on the last day of his fasting. Nothing bad was found in the examination of his blood.

During this experiment, Doctor Gayer, in addition to his routine work, performed other activities like bathing with cold and warm water, friction-bath, routine movements and markmanship with a gun.

At the end of the experiment, the committee of the above-mentioned five doctors published their opinion. They admitted that their beliefs regarding fasting were proved wrong. Even after the fasting of 31 days Doctor Gayer's body remained completely healthy and efficient. His weight, however, decreased. But these doctors accepted the fact that physical fitness does not depend only on weight.

Later on, Doctor Gayer regained his lost weight within only 22 days. The experiment of fasting had cleansed his body. And that was a bonus for him.

3. REJUVENATION BY FASTING

The case of the success of the science of fasting described below is interesting as well as important.

This is the case of a seventy years old gentleman who could be called, without exaggeration, a living museum of ailments. He was a perenial patient of cold, catarrh and sinusitis. He had been suffering from asthma for thirteen years. He had to spend many a sleepless night owing to a sudden, nocturnal attack of asthma followed by a short period during which he felt himself to be on the verge of death struggling for breathing. This gentleman had been suffering from impotence for about six years because of his enlarged prostate gland. Urinating was painful to him. The power of his hearing had been wearing out for the last several years. He considered medicines to be responsible for his ailment. He was tired of daily doses of new medicines. He had begun to abhor medicines. But he dared not think of giving up medicines for the fear of a severe asthma attack. He was admitted to the hospital five times. At last even the doctors washed their hands of his ailments. His ailments were considered as incurable.

He had previously applied nature cure also but not with full faith or efforts. It is obvious that the treatment taken without faith and sincerity does not prove beneficial.

At last, on insistence and under pressure of some friends he got himself admitted to Dr. MacFeddan's Nature Cure Centre. Having examined the patient's body, the doctor said, "His condition is serious. However, there is no reason to give up hope."

After having been admitted to the hospital, the patient was first of all instructed of discontinue taking medicines at all. This gave him a great shock. Expressing his apprehension he asked the doctor, "Sir, what shall I do if I suffer from an asthma attack again ?" The doctor replied, "If you continue taking medicines, you will never be cured. If you bear a few discomforts in the beginning, you will be benefitted in the end."

Amidst some doubts and fear, he commenced his fasting. On the very second day of fasting, he suffered from an asthma attack at 4 early in the morning. Immediately the doctor was sent for. The patient requested the doctor to give him medicine. Having examined him, the doctor said to him, "Have patience, the attack will cease within a short time." Having said so the doctor went away.

The patient thought that he had come to a wrong place as the doctors did not care to give him medicine to quieten the asthma attack nor did they give relief from it. He then blamed his fate and found faults with the doctors.

After some time, he got some relief from the attack, breathing became easier and he fell asleep.

His fasting continued. He did not suffer from the asthma attack again till he lived in the nature cure centre. Puss was no longer coming out of his nose and sinuses. Urinating became less painful. This was the sign of the improvement in the disorder of the prostate gland. On examination, it was found that the prostate gland had in fact shrunk.

At the end of the twenty-fifth day, the patient's condition improved significantly. He no longer experienced difficulty in urinating. Breathing was easy and smooth. It did not smell bad. Irrespective of all these apparent improvements, the doctor advised the patient to continue fast for a few more days.

The patient unhesitatingly abided by the doctor's advice. A miraculous event happened on the thirty-sixth day of his fasting. His deafness was suddenly cured. He was now able to hear the tick of a small clock which he used to keep near him.

His fasting ended after forty-two days. He was allowed to take planned food gradually. After some days, he resumed eating his usual food. Energy now began to flow rapidly into his body.

After returning home, he got another happy experience. He had regained his manliness. Having thus reached the climax of his joy and happiness, he wrote a letter to the doctor expressing his deep gratitude.

Unreal as it may appear, the above-mentioned case is indeed a fact. This case disproved the belief that fasting destroyed the strength and the beauty of the body. Restoration of hearing ability and manliness is an evidence of rejuvenation.

4. RECOVERY FROM FEVER

A tourist named Champaklal had gone to the Delwara Temples. He was to stay there for five to six days. On the very day of his arrival he got a severe fever. No medical treatment was available there. Coincidentally I was consulted.

I explained to him that fever itself was not a disease but it was only a symptom of some ailment in the body. When the energy of the body was trying to eliminate toxic elements accumulated in the body, an increase in the temperature of the body was natural. If one took food during that period, the energy of the body would be wasted. Then I advised him to stop taking food, to take warm water and rest. I also suggested that he clean his body with warm water applying a sponge twice a day.

He was hesitating to follow my advice. He had a desire for some medicine to gain quick relief. But that was not possible. At last, willingly or unwillingly, he became ready to accept the treatment as suggested by me.

The next morning, there was a decline in the temperature. He felt better. He had now developed faith in the treatment. He himself became ready to go without food for one more day. On the third day, the body exuded sweat and the temperature came down to normal.

Thereafter, he remained healthy during the rest of the days. Fasting had made his tour possible and easy.

5. FREEDOM FROM OBESITY AND STIFF JOINTS

Kanaiyalal was a dealer in ghee and butter at Hardoi (U. P.). He used to sit on a low table at his shop and taste the samples of ghee and butter he receiverd daily. Once he sat up on business, he would not rise from his seat. As a result, there was a gradual accumulaltion of fat in his body. His knee-joints became stiffer and stiffer day by day. His weight increased to 90 kg. As he was short in structure, this weight was considerably more for him. Along with this trouble, he now began to suffer from high blood pressure.

At last, he was put in such a state as rendered him unable to rise from the table without some one else's help. He now required somebody's support to reach his residence which was not very far from his shop. Walking made him extensively exhausted. At the slightest exertion he would experience difficulty in breathing.

He got himself treated by different doctors and vaidyas but the treatment gave him no benefit.

At last, he having been tired of various treatments, got himself admitted to 'Arogya Mandir', a nature cure centre at Gorakhpur (U. P.). He was allowed to take only warm water; he, however, was permitted to drink a little quantity of cold water at intervals, if he desired. The other treatments given to him consisted of daily massage and steam-bath once a day.

In the beginning, he was opposed to fasting. He was unable to remain hungry because he had formerly never missed a meal. Moreover, he was not mentally prepared for fasting. Here he had to live only on water.

At the end of ten days' fasting, his weight decreased by six kg. His knee-joints became a little free from stiffness. He was now able to step down from the cot and pace back and forth in the room.

After fifteen days, the doctor examined him and said that there was no objection if he ended his fast.

But Kanaiyalal expressed his desire to continue fasting as he felt better and there was no feeling of appetite.

This response of the patient gave the doctor a happy jolt.

Fasting was brought to an end exactly on the thirtieth day. His weight had decreased to 70 kg. Most of his ailments had disappeared. There was a significant dercrease in the blood pressure. Thereafter he was given simple food with a gradually increasing quantity. After about eight days he was able to walk for about a mile without undue fatigue or breathlessness.

6. RELIEF FROM COLD AND DIGESTIVE DISORDERS

Troubles caused by cold and indigestion are so common that there might be hardly a person who has been saved from them. Fasting brings an immediate remedy for these small ailments. Let us study an interesting case of a priest named Mathew Huven.

Mr. Mathew Huven always suffered from cold. The food taken by him was never normally digested. Medicines gave him a temporary relief. With the passing of a few days, these ailments reappeared with greater severity.

Being tired of current treatments, he decided to try fasting. He had occasionally heard of fasting but dared not put it into practice so far. But a sinking man catches at a straw. At last, he made up his mind to keep fasting.

He began fasting under the guidance of Dr. Bernarr MacFeddan. He spent the first ten to eleven days in restlessness. Toxic elements trying to come out of his body gave him much trouble. He began to think of giving up fasting, but comforted by Doctor MacFeddan and due to solace obtained by the company of other fasters, he put off the idea of abruptly abandoning fasting.

All his troubles suddenly subsided on the twelfth day of his fasting. Huven felt himself very energetic. He even began to do light physical exercises. He walked for two to three miles daily. He continued to do this for five days. Cold had already vanished before a few days.

At the end of his seventeen days' fasting, the doctor examined him and found that it was not necessary for him to continue fasting any longer. He was given only milk for nine days after the conclusion of his fasting. Within nine days, he regained 22 lb. out of 27 lb. of weight which he had lost during the period of fasting.

In addition to relief of cold and indigestion, other benefits which he derived were astonishing. His eye-sight improved considerably. His hair ceased falling. His skin regained lost lustre. Sluggishness and idleness completely vanished. He felt freshness and vitality in every part of his body.

7. DIARRHOEA AND ABDOMINAL PAIN

Navalbahen occasionally suffered from diarrhoea and abdominal pain. Medicines gave only temporary relief.

When she was tired of allopathic medicines, she would try Ayurvedic medicines. After some days, she would give up Ayurvedic medicines and turn to homeopathic medicines. This continued for a very long time. Once she suffered from chronic diarrhoea. Food taken by her would not remain in the stomach for long. She felt terrific weakness. In the end, she decided to try nature cure as a last resort. She called a well-known naturopath to her house.

The naturopath examined Navalbahen. Her intestines had become very weak. She was made to observe water-fast, although her body was extremely weak. During four days' fasting, the treatment given to her included warm water to drink, massage on the abdomen, wet earth on the abdomen and hip-bath. Due to this treatment, the organs of her abdomen got rest and strength. Thereafter she was given orange-juice mixed with water thrice a day. The juice-fast continued for some days. The treatment for the abdomen also continued along with fasting. Then she was given coconut water, mosambi juice, skimmed and very thin butter-milk etc. This experiment continued for fifteen days. Consequently, her intestines became strong and she was relieved of her abdominal pain.

They began to give her solid food gradually. At the initial stage, she was given fruits that contained no fibres. Then, after some time, raw vegetables, sprouted cereals and pulses were gradually added to her fruit-diet. Navalbahen was greatly pleased to find that all these foods were properly digested. After a few days, she was given a little quantity of cooked food which she could digest well.

8. FREEDOM FROM BODYACHE AND BACKACHE

Jivaraj Shah was about forty years old. He suffered from bodyache. He felt as if his muscles had been strained. Along with this trouble, he suffered from backache from time to time. Massage and tranquilizers gave him relief for some time, but he never felt absolutely relieved of pain. He was disgusted with this condition.

At last, he consulted a specialist. His stool, urine, blood, etc. were examined. Yet the cause of the disease could not be found. He followed the treatment prescribed by the doctor for a month, but there was no relief. Then he tried Ayurvedic and homeopathic treatment. Sometimes he got temporary relief but he was not completely relieved of his pains.

At last, he got himself admitted to a well-known nature cure centre where he was advised to observe fast. He was allowed to take only water and nothing else. He could not perceive why he was advised to fast for his ordinary ailments. The doctor explained that fasting was the most effective and unfailing remedy and therefore it should be tried.

He was given only warm water to drink. He was free to drink cold water at intervals. Hip-bath and enema were given to him on alternate days. At the initial stage, he was given steam-bath once a day. His pain had vanished of its own accord from the fourth day. For Jivaraj, it was a miracle. He himself now expressed his desire to continue the fast. He was made to fast for ten days. On the eleventh day, he broke his fast with fruit-juice. Thereafter he began to take very simple food. He resumed his usual meal after eight days. He never again complained of bodyache or backache.

9. CURE OF OBESITY, IRREGULAR MENSTRUATION AND INFERTILITY

Sudha was very fat. She experienced difficulty in breathing at the slightest exertion. When she approached me, she was so panting that she was unable to talk for two or three minutes.

Seven years ago, at the time of her marriage only slight obesity was present; but thereafter her weight began to increase. Her menstruation was proportionately less and irregular. She got it once after one and a half or two months. Prior to menstruation and during menstruation she suffered from abdominal pain. Menstruation would cease within only two days. She was childless so far. She had tried a number of remedies but in vain.

Doctors advised her to reduce her weight. They were of the opinion that reduction of weight would eliminate her troubles and make conception possible. Following the doctors' advice she tried to reduce her weight by eating less and observing an occasional fast. But this experiment proved ineffective. As she was tired of such fruitless experiments she left them.

After narrating the history of her ailments, she stated that she had read something on fasting and that she desired to keep long fasting under my guidance.

I told her that fasting was not necessary for reducing weight and added that proper and planned food habits also would give the expected benefits. But Sudha was firm in her determination of keeping a fast. At the initial stage I gave her only fruits and fruit-juices for four days. Other treatments included enema once a day and hip-bath with cold and warm water. Thereafter she embarked upon waterfasting. After the fasting of eight days, she got menstruation in which clotted blood was expelled in considerable proportion. As this had never happened previously, she became so panicky that she thought of abandoning fasting.

I explained to her that the extraction of clotted blood was a good sign showing that the uterus had become clear of toxins. I also persuaded her to continue her fasting for some more days so that her weight problem might be solved.

There was a considerable reduction in her weight at the end of fifteen days' fasting. Then she was gradually brought to taking her usual food. She was advised to observe a fast from time to time, stay on fruit-juices for some time, and take fruits and raw vegetables in her daily diet.

After a few months, when she came to me, I found her in a proportionate shape. With a smile on her face she told me that after the treatment given by me, her menstruation had been regular. She admitted that whatever benefit she got was due to fasting. She informed me that she had been pregnant for four months. She added that she continued taking food-items as suggested by me and would continue doing so.

10. CURE OF BURNING MICTURITION

Vinod was thirty years old. He had been suffering from burning micturition for the last two to two and a half years. He frequently got the sensation of urination and could not wait. If there was no facility or place for urinating, burning would increase and he would suffer abdomenal pain. As he lived in Mumbai, it was very difficult for him to get a suitable place for urinating whenever he got the sensation, which was very frequent. Also he had the complaints of headache and constipation. He had been consulting doctors and vaidyas for the past two years. He took their treatment but there was no improvement in his condition.

Being tired of medicines, he came to me as a last resort. Having listened to his history, I advised him to observe water-fast for a few days. He immediately followed my advice.

Along with fasting he was given enema and hip-bath every day. Wet earth was also put on his abdomen.

Within five or six days he was relieved of burning micturition. Encouraged by this result, he expressed his desire to continue fasting. At the end of his ten days' fasting, he was given orange-juice. Thereafter he was given juice-diet for four days. He was advised to take modified (as suggested) food-items gradually. These modified food-items included vegetable-soup. He was advised to keep a fast once a week.

After about a month when Vinod came to me, he was completely relieved of his ailments.

11. MALARIA IS CURED

A year ago Mr. Devakiprasad Pande, a tea-merchant of Mumbai, went to Assam for business purpose. There was a wild thicket around the bungalow where he put up. There was a small pond nearby. Mr. Pande was fascinated by the pleasant atmosphere and natural beauty. But there was a great nuisance of mosquitoes. He could not get good sleep at night. In the morning when he got up, he experienced fatigue and sluggishness. He stayed there for a week and each day he experienced fatigue and sluggishness in the morning. Then he got fever. He took medicine and when the fever subsided, he returned to Mumbai. But at Mumbai he was again attacked by fever.

The doctor diagnosed the fever as malaria and prescribed the medicines. Devakiprasad was so engrossed in his business activities that he could not take medicines regularly. He had a relapse of fever. This time the symptoms of fever were very severe. He got fever with rigors. He suffered from a severe headache along with fever. He vomitted at times. He started taking current medicines which lessened the severeness of fever, nevertheless he now began to get fever on alternate days.

Devakiprasad consulted a number of doctors. He tried the treatment by hakims and vaidyas. Occasionally, some medicine gave him some relief for some time but he was not cured of malaria.

Once a man of his acquaintance brought him to me. The patient's body was completely feeble. His face was pale, his eyes protruded and he was coughing at intervals. On examination, it was found that his spleen had been enlarged and morbidly sensitive.

As the condition was serious, I advised him to get himself admitted to a hospital and take modern treatment. But Devakiprasad, who was tired of medicines, was not prepared to try medicines again. He insisted on taking naturopathic treatment.

I advised him to fast. In the beginning, as a preparatory procedure he was given only liquid food for five days. During that period, he was given fruit and vegetable juices and leafy vegetable-soup. The physical treatment given to him included enema on every third day, steam-bath and wet earth to be put on his abdomen. This treatment gave him some relief of headache.

His real fasting commenced on the sixth day. He was advised to take warm water four or five times a day and cold water at intervals if he felt thirsty. He was allowed to add a little lemon or orange juice to the water as he desired once or twice a day.

The fever was under control after only four days of fasting. He now rarely coughed. He himself now felt more energetic than ever before.

After the eighth day of his fasting, the fever completely subsided. I advised him to continue fasting for a few days more even though he had lost as much weight as 5 kg.

On the twelfth day, he complained of nervousness, vomit sensation and nausea. His breathing was fast and pulse irregular. When he vomitted a lot, he was relieved of most of the painful symptoms. I thought that it was the proper stage when fasting should be ended. He had no relapse of fever during the last four days. He was again advised to have fruit and vegetable juices for diet. All his troubles subsided before he went to bed at night. He began to breathe normally and his heart-beats were regular.

After having kept him on juice-diet for two days, he was allowed to take solid food gradually. There was a gradual change in the type and quantity of food and on the eighth day he was permitted to resume his usual food. He was advised to take simple food and observe a fast once a week as a precaution.

Two months later, when I had a sudden meeting with him, I saw that he was very cheerful. Grasping my hands with his own, he stated that he had no relapse of fever and was feeling much better.

12. APPENDICITIS IS CURED

Sheela had been suffering from abdominal pain from time to time for one year. She had occasional nausea and sometimes vomitted. Medicines gave her some relief but the trouble did not completely vanish. At last, the family doctor told her that he suspected appendicitis, and advised her to consult a surgeon immediately. X-ray was taken and the surgeon advised her for an immediate operation. He stated that there was no other remedy except the operation. Taking his letter of recommendation, she went to the hospital and got the date fixed for the operation. The operation was to take place exactly after fifteen days.

Two or three days later, all of a sudden Sheela's father had to go to his native place. Before going he had told Sheela that if he did not turn up until the date of the operation, another date should be fixed for it.

In the absence of her father, Sheela got a severe abdominal pain. She approached me with a view to getting immediate relief and other treatment, if any.

I showed my unwillingness to take her case saying that the appendix is not essential for the body and that no risk was involved in its surgical removal.

The gentleman who had accompanied her told me that they had already decided for the operation but that the date for it was due after a few days and as she had a continuous abdominal pain, it would be better if some treatment was given to her for relief.

I advised her to begin fasting immediately. She was to take warm water four or five times a day. The other remedies which I suggested to her included fomentation with cold and hot water, and placing of wet earth on the abdomen. She got some relief. From the fourth day she began taking hip-bath with cold and hot water as per my advice. Within a week her abdominal pain subsided.

She was made to give up fasting after eight days and allowed to take juice-diet.

In the meantime, Sheela's father returned from his native place. Sheela was so relieved of her abdominal pain that all were in dilemma whether she should undergo the operation. After discussing the matter among themselves, they decided to call on the surgeon again. The surgeon found that there was relief of external symptoms. Moreover, she felt no pain when a definite part of the abdomen was pressed. He took the X-ray of her abdomen again and examined her fully. The report of the examination was so good that the surgeon opined that there was no need of operation.

13. CONCLUSION

Our ancestors and ancient physicians had made a deep study of the subject of preventive medicine, i.e., how to maintain good health. They had certainly realized that giving rest to the digestive system was inevitable for preservation of good health. They also had realized that people would not be willingly ready to abandon food. This was the reason why those far-sighted people gave religious significance to fasting.

There are good scientific reasons for fruit-diet, salt-less-diet (alunavrata). The minerals and vitamins which we do not get from our usual meals are available from fruit-diet. Salt which is very harmful to the body has no place in the meals taken by those who observe religious 'alunavrata' or 'ayambils'. We indeed bow our heads to those ancient physicians who possessed deep under-standing regarding health. The rules of health formulated by them are a blessing to mankind. They were in true sense watchmen of public health. It has been repeatedly mentioned in Indian medical books that if voluntary diet-restriction is followed, no medicine is necessary; while without dietary restriction no medicine can prove effective.

The modern science of medicine has taken a complete diversion from the old attitudes. Dazzled by manifestation of scientific discoveries, man of today has begun to lose his faith in religion with the result that he has abandoned traditional food habits. Men of modern medical science have taken advantage of human weakness. They thought that people would prefer any treatment which allowed them to eat whatever they liked. This thought goaded them to discover new medicines, and treatment by medicines became popular. These medicines have encouraged men to do whatever they like. At present, the condition of health is so much deteriorated that unless a red signal in the form of fasting and regimen is held before the people, the future of public health will be dark.

It needs to be remembered that fasting is not a means of competition and imitation. Today we find an excess of fasting during religious festivals. There is as if a fasting competition during the Paryushan festival of the Jains. A fasting of two months or more may possibly lead to disastrous consequences.

There can only be two aims of fasting : (1) Gaining health and (2) mental or spiritual development. Beasts and birds instinctively avoid taking food to get rid of illness. Man guided by logic has suppressed this instinct. Loss of appetite is a prominent symptom of almost every disease. Loss of appetite, which is a natural signal, indicates that the body does not require food. But man gifted with logic considers loss of appetite as an independent disease !

Man needs to have a second thought on his impulsive indications. Normally, a fast ranging from two to three days to one month is sufficient to regain health. A fast in excess of it is not a fast but starvation which is injurious to health. It is desirable that a fast of more than ten or twelve days should be observed under the recommendation and supervision of an experienced physician.

One cannot, at one's own will, keep a mental or spiritual fast. A truly religious person hardly realizes that he is in need of food; on the other hand, modern religious persons announce in advance that they will keep a fast of certain days. It is foolishness to declare in advance the period of fasting when one does not know in advance how many days of fasting are required. It is not necessary to keep fasting of 108 days or more for a religious purpose. The purpose of fasting is to keep the body fit so that religious activities can be continued without interruption.

Published by Navneet Publications (India) Ltd., Dantali, Gujarat.
Printed by   Shreeji Offset, 99, Amrut Industrial Estate, Ahm.-4

It is no exaggeration to say that

WHEAT GRASS IS THE PANACEA ON THE EARTH

- Are you disgusted with medicines? Are you apprehensive of their side-effects?
- Has your disease persisted in spite of taking a number of medicines?
- Do you want to provide your body with all essential vitamins and minerals in their natural and live form?
- Do you wish to remain always healthy?

THEN RESORT TO WHEAT GRASS

- Wheat grass enhances the natural resistance power of the body against disease.
- The chlorophyll present in wheat grass closely resembles 'hemin' of the human blood. It is not surprising that dieticians call wheat grass juice 'green blood.'
- A number of instances show that wheat grass juice can cure even cancer!

    Take wheat grass for just three weeks. Your diseases will disappear under the powerful curative influence of wheat grass. Your body will be filled with new vigour, your eyes will shine with lustre, your cheeks will show a rosy tinge and your skin will exude youth.

Salient features of this book :

- Complete, step by step instructions about growing wheat grass at your own home.
- Practical hints about the method of extraction and dosage of wheat grass juice.
- Full instructions about the use of wheat grass in a number of diseases.
- Case histories of successful use of wheat grass.

E 12